THIS SPAC

_____

_____

MY WELLNESS
SPACE
SEL Journal

"Socially and emotionally well children become thriving adults who realize their dreams."

Created by Eboni Bell, Ed.D
School Counselor & SEL Expert

Space for Me LLC
An Imprint of Space for Me LLC

Space for Me LLC
Fl 9 c/o wework
Charlotte, NC 28202
www.SpaceForMeConsulting.com

Author:
Eboni M Bell, Ed.D

Affirm Yourself Each Day

I AM COURAGEOUS

I AM LOVED

I AM BOLD

I AM WORTHY

I AM HEALTHY

I MAKE GOOD DECISIONS

I CONTRIBUTE TO MY COMMUNITY

I WILL SUCCEED

Purpose of Journal

The "My Wellness Space Journal" is designed to lead scholars on a journey of wellness through journaling, emotional discovery, and reflection on social emotional learning topics. This journal aids educators in social emotional skill-building efforts to increase self-awareness, academic achievement, and positive behaviors in and out of the classroom. Scholars begin with a wellness check-in. On these pages, scholars find space to share thoughts and emotions through written and artistic expression. In the next section, scholars have the opportunity to share what they know about the social emotional learning topic of the day, what they want to know, and to reflect on what they learn after the lesson is presented. The journal is most useful as a supplemental tool, during social emotional learning lessons, in restorative circles, or in small group settings. The "My Wellness Space Journal" is a safe space of self-reflection.

Contents

Introduction to Social Emotional Learning

1. Definition of SEL
2. Core Competencies of SEL

Section 1 - JOURNAL SPACE

1. Wellness Check-In
2. Hot Topic of the Day

Section 2 - SEL SPACE

1. SEL Focus
2. What I Know
3. What I Want to Know
4. What I Learned

Introduction to Social Emotional Learning

Definition of Social Emotional Learning

Social Emotional Learning (SEL) is a process that helps students improve academic and personal success, build character, increase empathy, identify and properly manage emotions, develop healthy relationships, and make wise decisions.

Five Core Competencies of SEL

1) self-awareness
2) self-management
3) responsible decision-making
4) social awareness
5) relationship skills

CASEL Quote on Benefits of SEL

"The benefits of social and emotional learning (SEL) are well-researched, with evidence demonstrating that an education that promotes SEL yields positive results for students, adults, and school communities." Casel.org

SEL Competencies Defined

1) self-awareness

The ability to be aware of your own thoughts, emotions, body and behaviors.

2) self-management

The ability to effectively manage one's own thoughts, emotions, body and behaviors.

3) responsible decision-making

The capacity to make caring, constructive and responsible decisions about your thoughts, emotions, body and behaviors.

4) social awareness

The ability to empathize, appreciate and understand the perspectives of others.

5) relationship skills

The ability to establish and maintain healthy relationships with others.

SEL Goal-Setting

Set a personal goal for each SEL competency.

1) self-awareness

2) self-management

3) responsible decision-making

4) social awareness

5) relationship skills

3

SECTION 1

JOURNAL SPACE

Use this section to:

- Do your wellness check-in.
- Identify your emotion of the day.
- Share what's on your mind.
- Journal your thoughts.
- Doodle or Draw.

Wellness Check-In

On a scale of 1-10, indicate how you feel today. Then, indicate an emotion that represents why you chose that number.

 my number

_____ my emotion

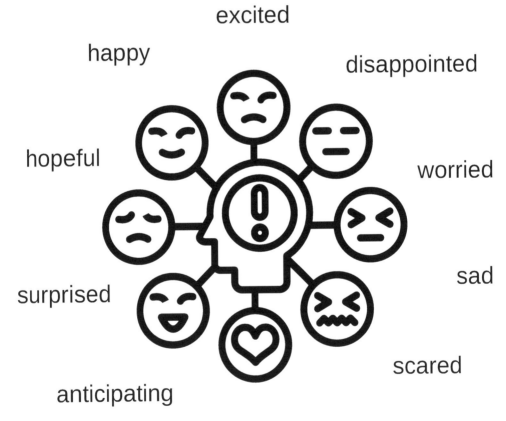

excited

happy

disappointed

hopeful

worried

surprised

sad

anticipating

scared

loved

angry

Hot Topic of the Day

What's on your mind today?
What's occupying space in your brain?
Use this space to write or draw and...

Wellness Check-In

On a scale of 1-10, indicate how you feel today. Then, indicate an emotion that represents why you chose that number.

my number

_____ my emotion

excited

happy

disappointed

hopeful

worried

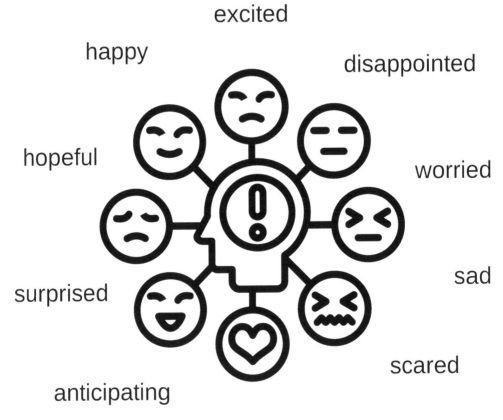

surprised

sad

anticipating

scared

loved

angry

Hot Topic of the Day

What's on your mind today?
What's occupying space in your brain?
Use this space to write or draw and...

LET IT OUT.

Wellness Check-In

On a scale of 1-10, indicate how you feel today. Then, indicate an emotion that represents why you chose that number.

 my number

_____ my emotion

excited

happy

disappointed

hopeful

worried

surprised

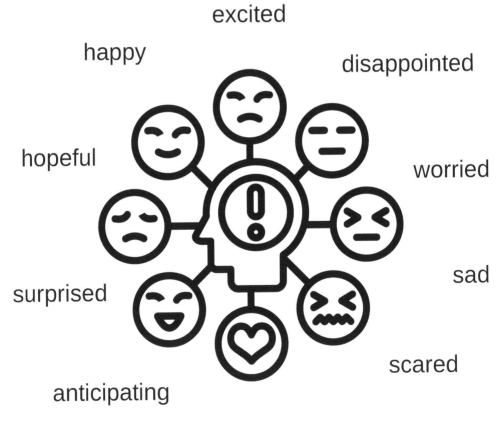

sad

anticipating

scared

loved

angry

Hot Topic of the Day

What's on your mind today?
What's occupying space in your brain?
Use this space to write or draw and...

Wellness Check-In

On a scale of 1-10, indicate how you feel today. Then, indicate an emotion that represents why you chose that number.

 my number

_____ my emotion

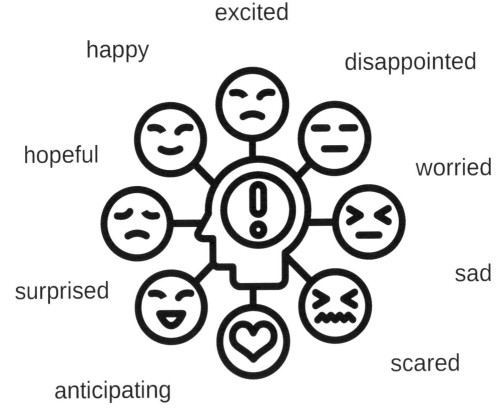

excited

happy

disappointed

hopeful

worried

surprised

sad

anticipating

scared

loved   angry

Hot Topic of the Day

What's on your mind today?

What's occupying space in your brain?

Use this space to write or draw and...

LET IT OUT.

Wellness Check-In

On a scale of 1-10, indicate how you feel today. Then, indicate an emotion that represents why you chose that number.

my number

_____ my emotion

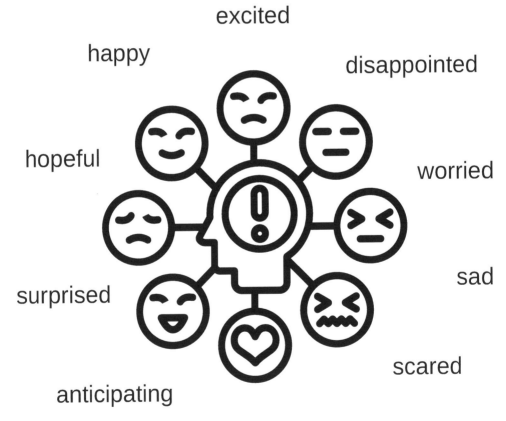

excited

happy

disappointed

hopeful

worried

surprised

sad

anticipating

scared

loved   angry

14

Hot Topic of the Day

What's on your mind today?

What's occupying space in your brain?

Use this space to write or draw and...

Wellness Check-In

On a scale of 1-10, indicate how you feel today. Then, indicate an emotion that represents why you chose that number.

 my number

_____ my emotion

excited

happy

disappointed

hopeful

worried

surprised

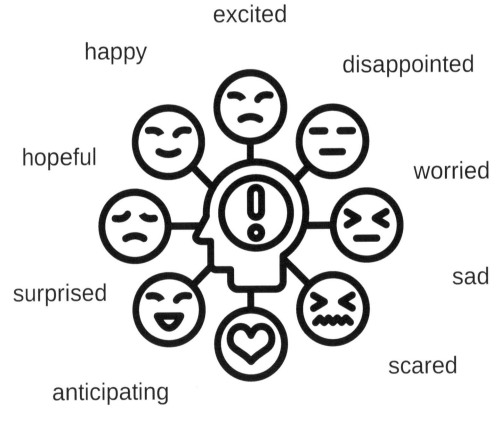

sad

scared

anticipating

loved   angry

Hot Topic of the Day

What's on your mind today?
What's occupying space in your brain?
Use this space to write or draw and...

Wellness Check-In

On a scale of 1-10, indicate how you feel today. Then, indicate an emotion that represents why you chose that number.

 my number

_____ my emotion

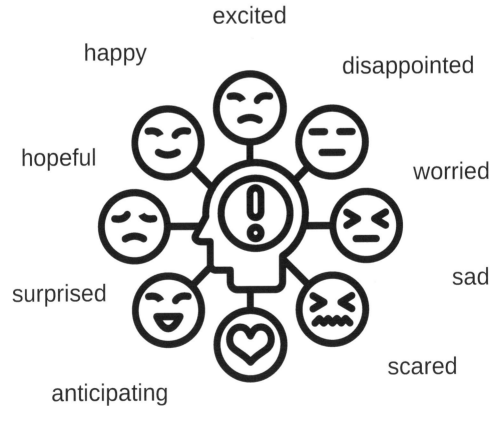

excited

happy

disappointed

hopeful

worried

surprised

sad

anticipating

scared

loved

angry

Hot Topic of the Day

What's on your mind today?

What's occupying space in your brain?

Use this space to write or draw and...

Wellness Check-In

On a scale of 1-10, indicate how you feel today. Then, indicate an emotion that represents why you chose that number.

 my number

_____ my emotion

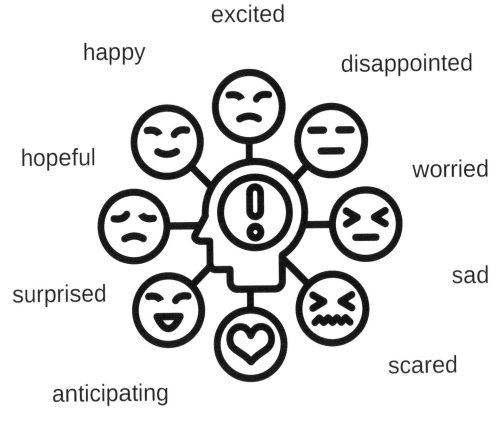

excited

happy

disappointed

hopeful

worried

surprised

sad

anticipating

scared

loved

angry

20

Hot Topic of the Day

What's on your mind today?

What's occupying space in your brain?

Use this space to write or draw and...

LET IT OUT.

Wellness Check-In

On a scale of 1-10, indicate how you feel today. Then, indicate an emotion that represents why you chose that number.

my number

_____ my emotion

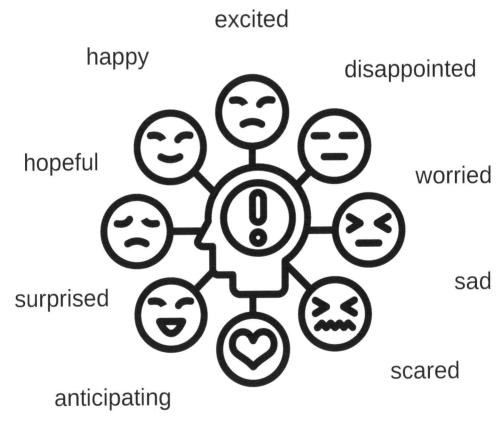

excited

happy

disappointed

hopeful

worried

surprised

sad

anticipating

scared

loved

angry

Hot Topic of the Day

What's on your mind today?

What's occupying space in your brain?

Use this space to write or draw and...

Wellness Check-In

On a scale of 1-10, indicate how you feel today. Then, indicate an emotion that represents why you chose that number.

my number

_____ my emotion

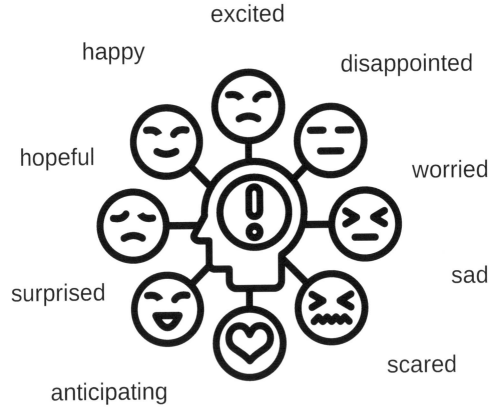

excited

happy

hopeful

disappointed

worried

surprised

sad

anticipating

scared

loved

angry

Hot Topic of the Day

What's on your mind today?
What's occupying space in your brain?
Use this space to write or draw and...

Wellness Check-In

On a scale of 1-10, indicate how you feel today. Then, indicate an emotion that represents why you chose that number.

 my number

_____ my emotion

excited

happy

disappointed

hopeful

worried

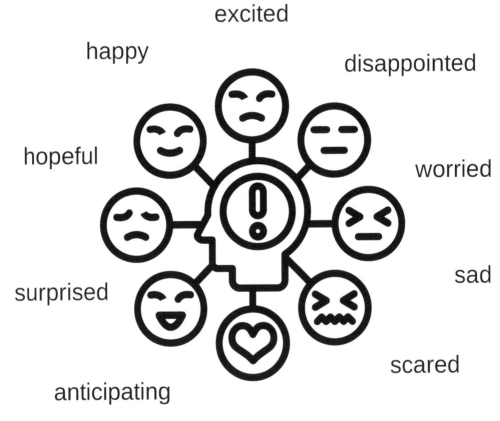

sad

surprised

scared

anticipating

angry

loved

Hot Topic of the Day

What's on your mind today?
What's occupying space in your brain?
Use this space to write or draw and...

Wellness Check-In

On a scale of 1-10, indicate how you feel today. Then, indicate an emotion that represents why you chose that number.

my number

_____ my emotion

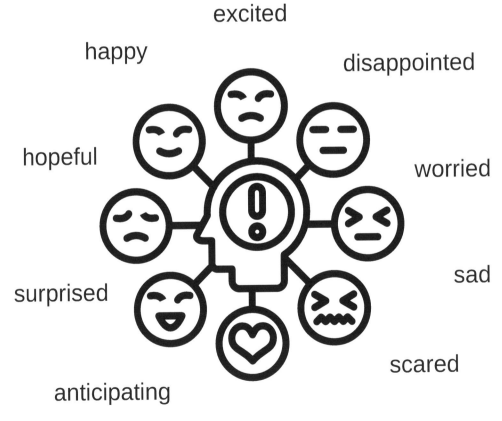

excited

happy

disappointed

hopeful

worried

surprised

sad

anticipating

scared

loved   angry

Hot Topic of the Day

What's on your mind today?
What's occupying space in your brain?
Use this space to write or draw and...

LET IT OUT.

Wellness Check-In

On a scale of 1-10, indicate how you feel today. Then, indicate an emotion that represents why you chose that number.

my number

_____ my emotion

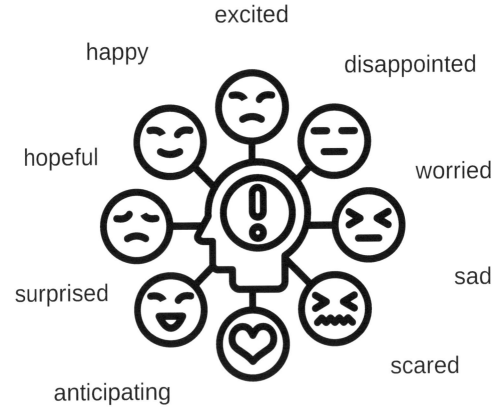

excited

happy

disappointed

hopeful

worried

surprised

sad

anticipating

scared

loved

angry

Hot Topic of the Day

What's on your mind today?

What's occupying space in your brain?

Use this space to write or draw and...

Wellness Check-In

On a scale of 1-10, indicate how you feel today. Then, indicate an emotion that represents why you chose that number.

[   ] my number

_____ my emotion

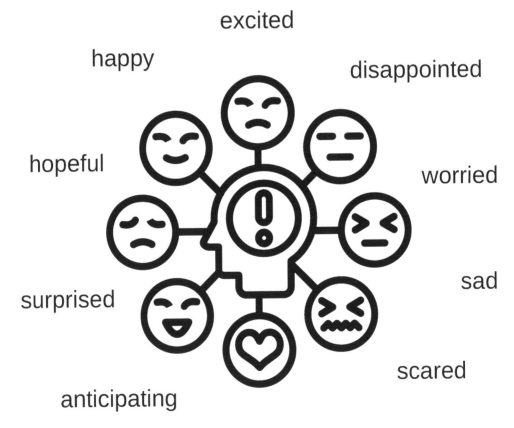

excited

happy

disappointed

hopeful

worried

surprised

sad

anticipating

scared

loved

angry

Hot Topic of the Day

What's on your mind today?

What's occupying space in your brain?

Use this space to write or draw and...

Wellness Check-In

On a scale of 1-10, indicate how you feel today. Then, indicate an emotion that represents why you chose that number.

☐ my number

_____ my emotion

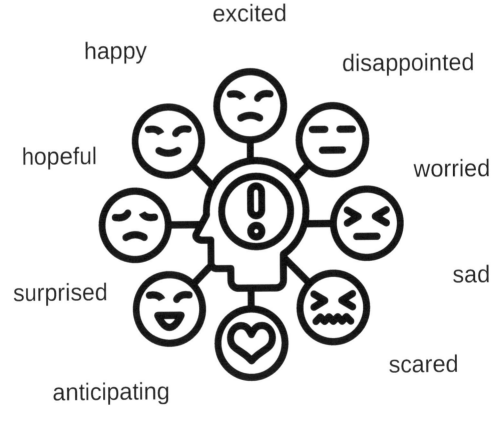

excited

happy

disappointed

hopeful

worried

surprised

sad

anticipating

scared

loved

angry

Hot Topic of the Day

What's on your mind today?

What's occupying space in your brain?

Use this space to write or draw and...

LET IT OUT.

Wellness Check-In

On a scale of 1-10, indicate how you feel today. Then, indicate an emotion that represents why you chose that number.

my number

_____ my emotion

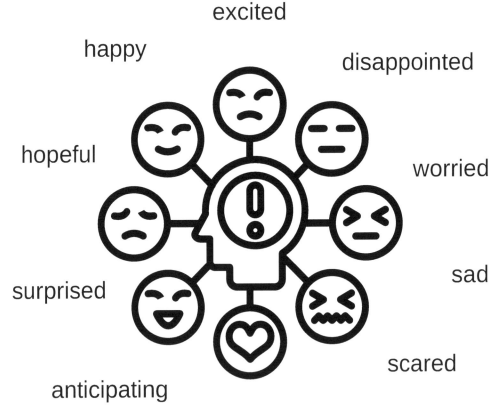

excited

happy

disappointed

hopeful

worried

surprised

sad

anticipating

scared

loved

angry

Hot Topic of the Day

What's on your mind today?

What's occupying space in your brain?

Use this space to write or draw and...

Wellness Check-In

On a scale of 1-10, indicate how you feel today. Then, indicate an emotion that represents why you chose that number.

my number

_____ my emotion

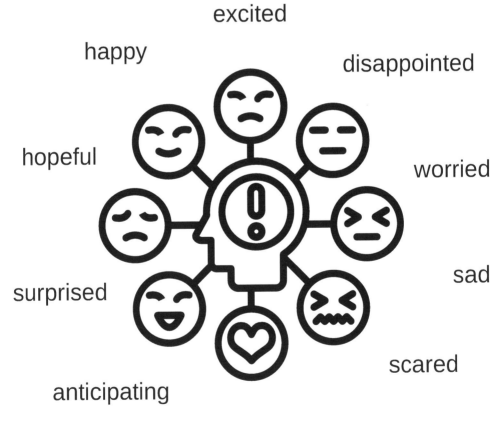

excited

happy

disappointed

hopeful

worried

surprised

sad

anticipating

scared

loved

angry

Hot Topic of the Day

What's on your mind today?

What's occupying space in your brain?

Use this space to write or draw and...

Wellness Check-In

On a scale of 1-10, indicate how you feel today. Then, indicate an emotion that represents why you chose that number.

my number

_____ my emotion

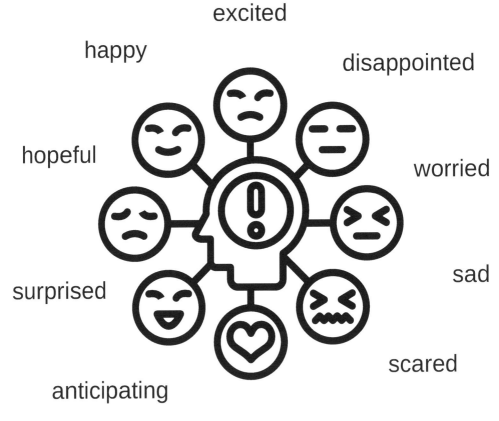

excited

happy

disappointed

hopeful

worried

surprised

sad

anticipating

scared

loved

angry

Hot Topic of the Day

What's on your mind today?
What's occupying space in your brain?
Use this space to write or draw and...

Wellness Check-In

On a scale of 1-10, indicate how you feel today. Then, indicate an emotion that represents why you chose that number.

my number

_____ my emotion

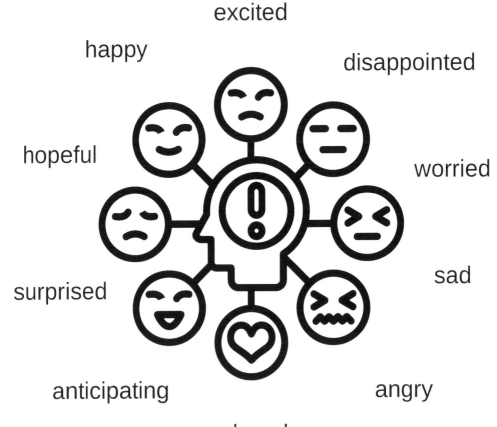

excited

happy

disappointed

hopeful

worried

surprised

sad

anticipating

angry

loved

Hot Topic of the Day

What's on your mind today?

What's occupying space in your brain?

Use this space to write or draw and...

Wellness Check-In

On a scale of 1-10, indicate how you feel today. Then, indicate an emotion that represents why you chose that number.

my number

_____ my emotion

excited

happy

disappointed

hopeful

worried

surprised

sad

anticipating

angry

loved

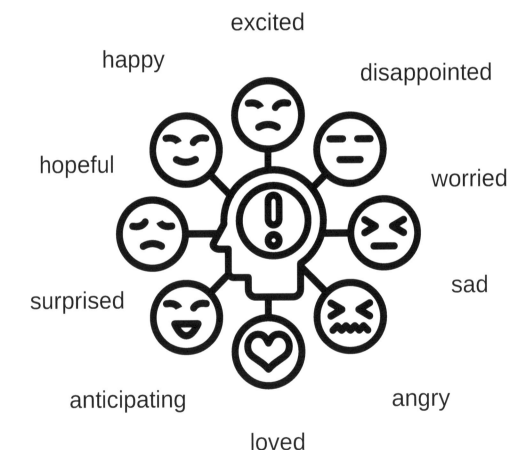

Hot Topic of the Day

What's on your mind today?

What's occupying space in your brain?

Use this space to write or draw and...

LET IT OUT.

Wellness Check-In

On a scale of 1-10, indicate how you feel today. Then, indicate an emotion that represents why you chose that number.

my number

_____ my emotion

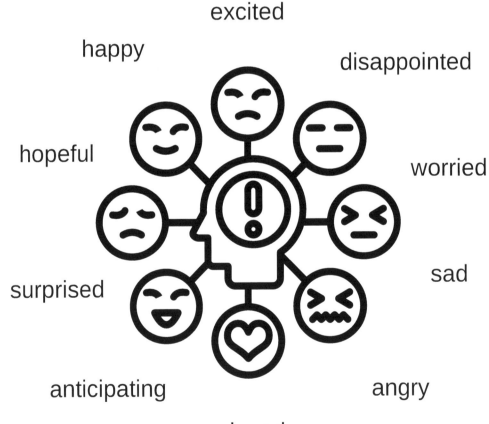

excited

happy

disappointed

hopeful

worried

surprised

sad

anticipating

angry

loved

Hot Topic of the Day

What's on your mind today?

What's occupying space in your brain?

Use this space to write or draw and...

Wellness Check-In

On a scale of 1-10, indicate how you feel today. Then, indicate an emotion that represents why you chose that number.

 my number

_____ my emotion

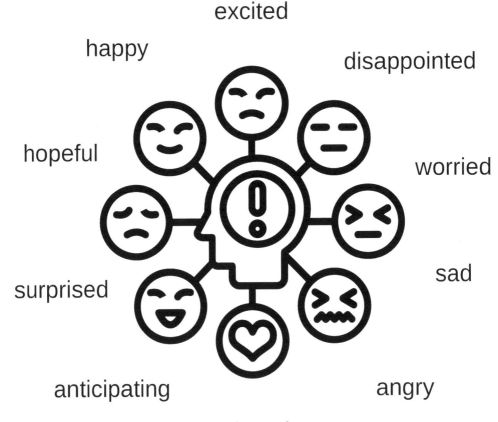

excited

happy

disappointed

hopeful

worried

surprised

sad

anticipating

angry

loved

Hot Topic of the Day

What's on your mind today?

What's occupying space in your brain?

Use this space to write or draw and...

LET IT OUT.

Wellness Check-In

On a scale of 1-10, indicate how you feel today. Then, indicate an emotion that represents why you chose that number.

[ ] my number

_____ my emotion

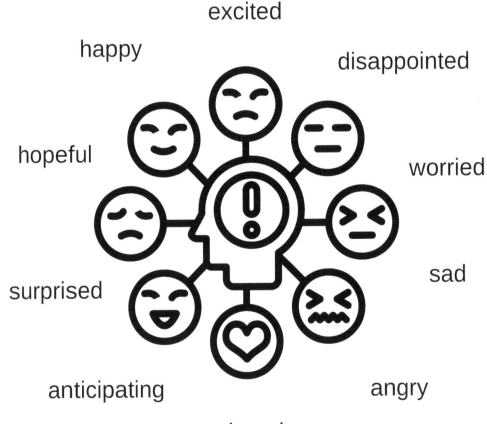

excited

happy

disappointed

hopeful

worried

surprised

sad

anticipating

angry

loved

Hot Topic of the Day

What's on your mind today?

What's occupying space in your brain?

Use this space to write or draw and...

SECTION 2

SEL SPACE

Use this section to:

- Take notes on the SEL topic.
- State the SEL topic of the day.
- Note what you already know about the topic.
- Note what else you want to know about the topic.
- Note what you learned about the topic, after the lesson.

SEL Focus

List the topic or theme of the lesson.

What I Know

What do you currently know about the SEL lesson topic? Do you have any personal experience with the topic? Brainstorm here.

What I Want to Know

Take notes and ask questions about the SEL topic.

What I Learned

What new knowledge did you gain from the lesson? How can you use it to help you in everyday life?

SEL Focus

List the topic or theme of the lesson.

What I Know

What do you currently know about the SEL lesson topic? Do you have any personal experience with the topic? Brainstorm here.

What I Want to Know

Take notes and ask questions about the SEL topic.

What I Learned

What new knowledge did you gain from the lesson? How can you use it to help you in everyday life?

SEL Focus

List the topic or theme of the lesson.

What I Know

What do you currently know about the SEL lesson topic? Do you have any personal experience with the topic? Brainstorm here.

What I Want to Know

Take notes and ask questions about the SEL topic.

What I Learned

What new knowledge did you gain from the lesson? How can you use it to help you in everyday life?

SEL Focus

List the topic or theme of the lesson.

What I Know

What do you currently know about the SEL lesson topic? Do you have any personal experience with the topic? Brainstorm here.

What I Want to Know

Take notes and ask questions about the SEL topic.

What I Learned

What new knowledge did you gain from the lesson? How can you use it to help you in everyday life?

SEL Focus

List the topic or theme of the lesson.

What I Know

What do you currently know about the SEL lesson topic? Do you have any personal experience with the topic? Brainstorm here.

What I Want to Know

Take notes and ask questions about the SEL topic.

What I Learned

What new knowledge did you gain from the lesson? How can you use it to help you in everyday life?

SEL Focus

List the topic or theme of the lesson.

What I Know

What do you currently know about the SEL lesson topic? Do you have any personal experience with the topic? Brainstorm here.

What I Want to Know

Take notes and ask questions about the SEL topic.

What I Learned

What new knowledge did you gain from the lesson? How can you use it to help you in everyday life?

SEL Focus

List the topic or theme of the lesson.

What I Know

What do you currently know about the SEL lesson topic? Do you have any personal experience with the topic? Brainstorm here.

What I Want to Know

Take notes and ask questions about the SEL topic.

What I Learned

What new knowledge did you gain from the lesson? How can you use it to help you in everyday life?

SEL Focus

List the topic or theme of the lesson.

What I Know

What do you currently know about the SEL lesson topic? Do you have any personal experience with the topic? Brainstorm here.

What I Want to Know

Take notes and ask questions about the SEL topic.

What I Learned

What new knowledge did you gain from the lesson? How can you use it to help you in everyday life?

SEL Focus

List the topic or theme of the lesson.

What I Know

What do you currently know about the SEL lesson topic? Do you have any personal experience with the topic? Brainstorm here.

What I Want to Know

Take notes and ask questions about the SEL topic.

What I Learned

What new knowledge did you gain from the lesson? How can you use it to help you in everyday life?

SEL Focus

List the topic or theme of the lesson.

What I Know

What do you currently know about the SEL lesson topic? Do you have any personal experience with the topic? Brainstorm here.

What I Want to Know

Take notes and ask questions about the SEL topic.

What I Learned

What new knowledge did you gain from the lesson? How can you use it to help you in everyday life?

SEL Focus

List the topic or theme of the lesson.

What I Know

What do you currently know about the SEL lesson topic? Do you have any personal experience with the topic? Brainstorm here.

What I Want to Know

Take notes and ask questions about the SEL topic.

What I Learned

What new knowledge did you gain from the lesson? How can you use it to help you in everyday life?

SEL Focus

List the topic or theme of the lesson.

What I Know

What do you currently know about the SEL lesson topic? Do you have any personal experience with the topic? Brainstorm here.

What I Want to Know

Take notes and ask questions about the SEL topic.

What I Learned

What new knowledge did you gain from the lesson? How can you use it to help you in everyday life?

SEL Focus

List the topic or theme of the lesson.

What I Know

What do you currently know about the SEL lesson topic? Do you have any personal experience with the topic? Brainstorm here.

What I Want to Know

Take notes and ask questions about the SEL topic.

What I Learned

What new knowledge did you gain from the lesson? How can you use it to help you in everyday life?

SEL Focus

List the topic or theme of the lesson.

What I Know

What do you currently know about the SEL lesson topic? Do you have any personal experience with the topic? Brainstorm here.

What I Want to Know

Take notes and ask questions about the SEL topic.

What I Learned

What new knowledge did you gain from the lesson? How can you use it to help you in everyday life?

SEL Focus
List the topic or theme of the lesson.

What I Know

What do you currently know about the SEL lesson topic? Do you have any personal experience with the topic? Brainstorm here.

What I Want to Know

Take notes and ask questions about the SEL topic.

What I Learned

What new knowledge did you gain from the lesson? How can you use it to help you in everyday life?

SEL Focus

List the topic or theme of the lesson.

What I Know

What do you currently know about the SEL lesson topic? Do you have any personal experience with the topic? Brainstorm here.

What I Want to Know

Take notes and ask questions about the SEL topic.

What I Learned

What new knowledge did you gain from the lesson? How can you use it to help you in everyday life?

SEL Focus

List the topic or theme of the lesson.

What I Know

What do you currently know about the SEL lesson topic? Do you have any personal experience with the topic? Brainstorm here.

What I Want to Know

Take notes and ask questions about the SEL topic.

What I Learned

What new knowledge did you gain from the lesson? How can you use it to help you in everyday life?

SEL Focus

List the topic or theme of the lesson.

```

```

What I Know

What do you currently know about the SEL lesson topic? Do you have any personal experience with the topic? Brainstorm here.

SEL Focus
List the topic or theme of the lesson.

What I Know

What do you currently know about the SEL lesson topic? Do you have any personal experience with the topic? Brainstorm here.

SEL Focus

List the topic or theme of the lesson.

What I Know

What do you currently know about the SEL lesson topic? Do you have any personal experience with the topic? Brainstorm here.

What I Want to Know

Take notes and ask questions about the SEL topic.

What I Learned

What new knowledge did you gain from the lesson? How can you use it to help you in everyday life?

SEL Focus

List the topic or theme of the lesson.

What I Know

What do you currently know about the SEL lesson topic? Do you have any personal experience with the topic? Brainstorm here.

What I Want to Know

Take notes and ask questions about the SEL topic.

What I Learned

What new knowledge did you gain from the lesson? How can you use it to help you in everyday life?

SEL Focus

List the topic or theme of the lesson.

What I Know

What do you currently know about the SEL lesson topic? Do you have any personal experience with the topic? Brainstorm here.

What I Want to Know

Take notes and ask questions about the SEL topic.

What I Learned

What new knowledge did you gain from the lesson? How can you use it to help you in everyday life?

SEL Focus

List the topic or theme of the lesson.

What I Know

What do you currently know about the SEL lesson topic? Do you have any personal experience with the topic? Brainstorm here.

What I Want to Know

Take notes and ask questions about the SEL topic.

What I Learned

What new knowledge did you gain from the lesson? How can you use it to help you in everyday life?

SEL Focus

List the topic or theme of the lesson.

What I Know

What do you currently know about the SEL lesson topic? Do you have any personal experience with the topic? Brainstorm here.

What I Want to Know

Take notes and ask questions about the SEL topic.

What I Learned

What new knowledge did you gain from the lesson? How can you use it to help you in everyday life?

SEL Focus

List the topic or theme of the lesson.

What I Know

What do you currently know about the SEL lesson topic? Do you have any personal experience with the topic? Brainstorm here.

What I Want to Know

Take notes and ask questions about the SEL topic.

What I Learned

What new knowledge did you gain from the lesson? How can you use it to help you in everyday life?

SEL Focus

List the topic or theme of the lesson.

What I Know

What do you currently know about the SEL lesson topic? Do you have any personal experience with the topic? Brainstorm here.

What I Want to Know

Take notes and ask questions about the SEL topic.

What I Learned

What new knowledge did you gain from the lesson? How can you use it to help you in everyday life?

SEL Focus

List the topic or theme of the lesson.

What I Know

What do you currently know about the SEL lesson topic? Do you have any personal experience with the topic? Brainstorm here.

What I Want to Know

Take notes and ask questions about the SEL topic.

What I Learned

What new knowledge did you gain from the lesson? How can you use it to help you in everyday life?

SEL Focus

List the topic or theme of the lesson.

What I Know

What do you currently know about the SEL lesson topic? Do you have any personal experience with the topic? Brainstorm here.

Congratulations on
taking the wellness journey!

Made in the USA
Columbia, SC
16 February 2023

12546150R00063